Unabridged Book Review

"What a story of faith and survival. This book should be in every clinic, every doctor and dentist office, on the pulpit of every minister to help bring those who need it comfort and to remind those who trespass that they should not."

NIKKI GIOVANNI

World-renowned poet, writer, commentator, activist, educator, and one of Oprah Winfrey's living legends

I0169145

Love Poems from God

My Poems and Practical Exercises

By Mary Vasquez

Divinefulness Publishing

Love Your True Self

Divinefulness Publishing, Inc.
Chicago, IL

Thank you for choosing this Divinefulness Publishing, Inc., paperback.

As a bonus for reading this book, ***Love Poems from God: My Poems and Practical Exercises,*** join our email list, and you will receive Mary's song, "When Life Gets You Down, Get Up!" for FREE. See the last page for details. To hear a song clip go directly to our Website at divinefulns.us/MarysSongClip. Then share it.

Help Mary write her next book, ***Loving Me 101: Loving My Divinefulness,*** and receive advance notice about future online retreats. For details, see the "Connect with Mary Vasquez" page.

Published in the United States by
Divinefulness Publishing, Inc.
P.O. Box 34288, Chicago, IL 60634
DivinefulnessPublishing.com

Spiritual Books for People with Life-Altering Experiences, Loved Ones, and Care Providers
"Love Your True Self"

Author, editor, and interior designer: Mary Vasquez
Author photographs on cover: Mike Pocius
Cover design concept: Shawn Noel Simmons
Cover design: Vila Design
Original crucifix artwork: Sylvia Gierasimczuk
Artist's website: sylviagdesign.com
Layout: Elizabeth Fromm

The author is not a licensed doctor or therapist, and this book is not recommended as an alternative to
therapeutic counseling. She is someone just like you or your loved one who conquered the darkness. If
you or a loved one is suffering from post-traumatic stress or another anxiety illness and is not in therapy,
the author urges you to immediately seek professional help in your community. A Resources section
located in the back of this book can assist you in your search.

When using any of the information in this book for yourself, the author and publisher assume no
responsibility for your actions.

Library of Congress Control Number: 2015901890

A Rape Survivor's Spiritual Journey (Unabridged edition)

ISBN: 978-0-9886717-2-0 Unabridged Epub
ISBN: 978-0-9886717-4-4 Unabridged Kindle
ISBN: 978-0-9886717-6-8 Unabridged Paperback

Unabridged Ebook: First Edition, February 2015
Unabridged Paperback: First Edition, March 2015

Library of Congress Control Number: 2015918127

Love Poems from God (Abridged edition of A Rape Survivor's Spiritual Journey)

ISBN: 978-0-9886717-3-7 Abridged Epub
ISBN: 978-0-9886717-5-1 Abridged Kindle
ISBN: 978-0-9886717-7-5 Abridged Paperback

Abridged Ebook: First Edition, October 2015
Abridged Paperback: First Edition, November 2015

Dedicated to You
May your healing journey
take you far beyond
your hopes and dreams.

Contents

Preface

My biological father sexually abused me from about the age of five until I turned 13. During one of the darkest times in my life after the abuse, I lived at the YMCA in Chicago's Gold Coast in a room the size of a large walk-in closet and worked as a security guard in a River North condo building. That's when I was blessed with the remarkable experience and privilege of writing a book I never wanted to write.

It all started at The Leaven Center during a writers retreat for women in Lyons, Michigan, in January of 2005. I went there to find clarity and focus for writing my screenplay. When I returned, poem titles kept popping into my head and repeating themselves, like a two-year-old on a sugar high, until I wrote them down. As it turned out, the compiled poems tell my life story.

I now realize that God gave me these uplifting and dark poems to help me heal myself from my horrifying childhood. They were, literally and figuratively, a godsend. Even though I fought God pretty much all along the way, I knew that forging ahead was the only way out of my misery. I wish I knew then that holding onto my faith in God would lead me to conquer post-traumatic stress.

This abridged edition of *A Rape Survivor's Spiritual Journey: My Poems and Practical Exercises* contains only the uplifting poems with journal pages for readers to use. The unabridged version is available for purchase.

Whenever you are having a difficult time and need a quick dose of encouragement, I hope you will find this book inspiring. I pray one or more of these poems speaks to you and helps you in your healing process. Musically, spark your spirit with a free copy of my song, "When Life Gets You Down, Get Up!" See the last page of this book for details.

Acknowledgements

God's unconditional love, priceless faith, and infinite graces saved my life. Recently, long after I wrote this book, I struggled through the worst depression I ever experienced. My mind, senses, and spirit constantly wrestled with the bleak darkness, and my only consolation came during prayer.

Thank God I met William Rosado, another survivor, who helped me achieve a miraculous breakthrough. I still cannot believe I no longer suffer from post-traumatic stress (PTS) nor feel traumatized by flashbacks, and I finally feel normal. Read more about my breakthrough in the afterword.

My mother, God rest her soul, practiced what she preached. Actually, she never preached. Instead, she melted my heart with her gentle love and compassion. I wanted to grow up and be just like her because she was always smiling, laughing, and in a good mood. That's why as a little girl I read the Bible nonstop for hours even though I really didn't understand most of what I was reading. She already found the secret to happiness, and all I had to do was follow her lead.

She talked to everyone she met as if she had known them her entire life and never had a bad word to say about anybody. Our next-door neighbors, Max and Esther Friend, a wonderfully warm, elderly Jewish couple, were close to my family. My mother explained how they lived their faith in doing good works, respecting others, and going to their own church (temple), too. Their God was our God, too, she once told me. I remember one year when I gave them a Christmas card, they graciously accepted. I still feel like such an idiot.

My brother, Tony, and my youngest nephew, Eric, would be next. Thank you for your love and encouragement during the years I struggled in the bleak darkness and the long path that finally led to publishing this book.

Although one of my sisters, Mary Sarelli, passed away years ago, reconnecting with her children and their families has been such a blessing. Thank you all for your love and confidence in me and my publishing aspirations. I look forward to finding my sisters Lilly and Rosie Vasquez, the infant taken away by the state after their mother passed away, and my sister Maria del Consuelo Arvizu, too.

My best friend, Shawn Noel Simmons, has always supported me throughout my life and all my endeavors, and this book is no different. She conceptualized the book covers, too. Thank you, sister. I love you!

Generous with his WordPress knowledge and developer expertise, Edmund Dante Hamilton's contributions have been invaluable to Divinefulness Publishing, Inc. Thank you, my trusted friend.

I will never forget my fifth grade teacher, Mrs. Wisclek, formerly known as Miss Wisniewski. By encouraging class performances of short plays that my best friend and I wrote, she planted a seed of empowerment. When I finally started pursuing my passion for writing, that exhilarating memory of performing in her class with our mothers present confirmed that I found my passion.

Then, there's Ruth Mojica-Hammer, whom I met while working at WTTW-TV/Channel 11 (PBS) in Chicago when I attended Northeastern Illinois University. She urged me to pursue my passion for writing. Thank you, Ruth, for enthusiastically convincing me I was a gifted writer. Although my mother constantly supported my writing pursuits, I wasn't sure if she was doing it just because I was her daughter.

Thank you, Tina Nudo, for your friendship and encouragement while I finished writing this book. A very special thank you goes out to Cyndi Hefler, a close friend, whom I also met during those agonizing and joyful days. Always enthusiastic, she persuaded me to keep writing when I wasn't sure I had any business thinking I could write a book. Whenever I brought her the latest poems I wrote, she kept telling me how powerful and pure they were and insisted I keep writing. Cyndi's also responsible for including a short poem I almost omitted here, one she found compelling. I will always treasure my friendship with you both.

My first counselor at the YWCA in Chicago, Dawn Emmons-Julian, saved my life. While walking a fine line between losing and retaining my sanity and not letting my suicidal thoughts develop, she was the perfect balance of gentleness and a firm, no-nonsense approach to taking practical steps in my healing process. Thank you, Dawn, for saving my life. I will never forget you!

After Dawn had a stroke and left the YWCA, Lara Brooks became my therapist and wholeheartedly encouraged my writing, which at the time was more desire than story. She used to bring all kinds of poetry and literature to our therapy sessions. When I told Lara I wanted to write a screenplay, she suggested a writers retreat for women at the Leaven Center in Lyons, Michigan, where I became inspired to write this book.

Then there are Josephine Ruiz and Deslonde Parkinson of the YWCA. Thank you both for facilitating intimate group therapy sessions and nurturing us along the way. You not only created a safe place for us but also guided us as we made all our own decisions about acceptable and intolerable behavior in our group. Empowering us to do so helped us all begin to learn how to set our own boundaries.

Thank you, Elizabeth Fromm, for your diligent work on the layout of this book. Your passion for this project has meant the world to me. Thank you also for your dear friendship, which I will cherish forever.

True friends are there for you when you need them, a statement that sums up my friendship with Kevin Fitzpatrick. Thank you, Kevin, for your moral support during my struggles with the darkness over the years. I would also like to thank all of my other friends and family for their endless love.

The crucifix graphic by Sylvia Gierasimczuk is nothing less than stunning. Thank you, Sylvia, for this deeply spiritual piece that takes everyone's breath away and evokes an interior pain only a true artist can capture.

Thank you, Mike Pocius, for my flattering image on the cover and the author photo. Your photographic talent and friendship are exceptional. Gail Selleg, you're such a good friend. Thank you, so much, for asking Mike to share his artistic gift with me.

To the many survivors I have met, thank you for sharing your stories and good wishes. I pray God's love and peace will empower you to persevere as you continue following your healing path. May your lives far surpass all your hopes and dreams.

Introduction

Whether your spiritual journey leads you to Jesus, Adonai, or the divine creator by another name, please know I respect your spiritual nature and hope you will read this book, substituting the name of your higher power wherever I mention God or Jesus. God is love, and as pure love, He is always inclusive, and I believe that we should be, too.

God speaks to everyone. We just don't always listen. I know I don't. You will notice that some of the poems contain lines in italics. That's God talking. Those were the rare moments I was really listening. As you read the uplifting poems, feel God's awe-inspiring, unconditional love and hear his gentle whispers as they console and ignite your spirit.

If you struggle with self-injury, one inspirational poem, "The Truth," may elicit flashbacks. Although the ending is uplifting, you may want to consult your therapist before reading this poem.

As a survivor of childhood sexual abuse, my spiritual path has led me to experience the darkness of pure evil and the blinding brilliance of interior peace. For those who are ready to take a journey back in time with me through the darkness as well as the light, I offer the unabridged edition of this book, *A Rape Survivor's Spiritual Journey: My Poems and Practical Exercises*, with journal pages for readers to use.

Whenever you are having a difficult time and need a quick dose of encouragement, I hope you will find this book inspiring. I pray one or more of these poems speaks to you and helps you in your healing process. Musically, spark your spirit with a free copy of my song, "When Life Gets You Down, Get Up!" See the last page of this book for details.

Please also consider using the journal pages. Writing down my feelings and being able to go back and look at them with my therapist's help have been invaluable to me. As a child, pretending the abuse never happened helped me cope, but when I became an adult, it wasn't working anymore.

However, this book is not recommended as an alternative to therapeutic counseling. If you or a loved one is suffering from symptoms of post-traumatic stress (PTS) or another anxiety illness and is not in therapy, I urge you to immediately seek professional help in your community. Located in the back of this book, the Resources section can help you. I am not a licensed doctor or therapist. I am someone just like you or your loved one who has conquered the darkness and no longer suffers from PTS. For details, please read the afterword.

A Love Letter from God

Be still and know that I love you.
I will ALWAYS love you,
and nothing you've done
or will do can ever change that.

Your tears are my tears.
And your torments and heartaches
are mine, too.

Let me hold you in my arms
and cry with you.
Feel my love for you
in the warmth of your tears
for they come from me
because I live inside you.

Beneath the terror, numbness, and exhaustion,
I lie there waiting for you to call on me.
Talk to me: out loud, whisper, or speak to me
in the silence of your heart,
and I will always listen and comfort you:
know this and never doubt.

Your Journal: Write Your Letter to God

What would you like to tell God right now?

Return to Live!

You hate me.
That's okay,
but I still love you just the same.
I know that you're not you, AND you're in agony and pain.

I see you suffer and hear you cry.
I wish you'd turn to me,
and see me cry beside you
and hear my gentle plea.

Come back. Come back. Come back to me!
Let me hold you in my arms.
I loved you into life. Please let me love you one more time.
I'm here and love you SO much it makes me cry to see
you struggle all alone and no longer call on me.

Hate me. Yell and swear at me if that's exactly how you feel.
Just keep talking. Don't shut me out. I'm not going anywhere.
Go ahead. Do it. Right now. I'm always listening, you know.
Remember, you can hate me, but away I'll never go.

Return to me. Return to live
the life I meant for you,
and through your suffering and pain
you will find your life renewed.

Inspired by Ezekiel 18:32.

Your Journal: Changing Your Negative Self-Talk

You can begin to RETURN TO LIVE by changing the negative self-talk in your head. Start doing this by

1. Writing a list of at least five "I am…" daily affirmations. (For example, I am smart. I am talented. I am beautiful inside and out. I am a gift from God to the world. I am here for a reason.)

2. Writing another list of at least five positive self-talk sentences to replace your worst negative self-talk. After negative sentences, say, "That's wrong!" Then, read your positive ones. Be sure to read them at least once every day. Below are some examples.

    a. It's all my fault. That's wrong! All of the blame belongs to the criminal(s) who assaulted me.

    b. I'm a horrible person. That's wrong! I am a beautiful person who experienced a horrible crime.

    c. I don't deserve a better life. That's wrong! I deserve to live a life that surpasses all my hopes and dreams.

    d. I'll never amount to anything. That's wrong! I have the strength for everything through Him who empowers me. (Phil 4:13)

    e. I'll never be happy. That's wrong! I will make myself happy by enjoying life more.

Consider reading these affirmations in front of a mirror whenever possible or carrying them with you.

5

Hold Onto the Light

Come out of the darkness.
Come out and join me.
Here, take my hand. Don't be afraid.
Come out with me, please.

I won't leave you alone
as you come out of your night.
I promise you, YES, it will be alright.
No, I won't lie, you will see darkness again.

I can only remind you to reach out your hand.
And know I will pull you out again and again.
When you find yourself slipping into the dark of your night,
just remember to hold onto Me. Hold onto the light.

Your Journal: How to Hold Onto the Light in the Darkness

When you're in the darkness, how will you remember to
HOLD ONTO THE LIGHT?

Some ways you can HOLD ONTO THE LIGHT are by

Seeking professional help in your community. (See the Resources section in the back of this book.)

Letting trusted friends and family know you need their love and support.

Talking to God in prayer and asking for strength.

Reminding yourself to hang onto God like you would hang onto a capsized boat in the ocean during a storm.

Going out with trusted friends or family. You don't need to spend a lot of money. Go with them for a walk, a movie, or hang out at their place.

My Temple

My tiny temple.
My innocent spirit.
No rules.

He desecrated my temple.
He crushed my innocence.
He tortured my soul.

My new temple.
My new spirit.
God rules.

Your Journal: Finding God inside the Holy Temple of Your Body

The Spirit of God lives and breathes with me.
I breathe with the Spirit.
I AM one with the Spirit.
I AM God's Spirit.

At all times and in all places, the Spirit of God lives and breathes inside me.
I breathe with the Spirit.
I AM one with the Spirit.
I AM God's Spirit.

The Spirit of God empowers me with the strength to
[insert your greatest challenge here].
I breathe with the Spirit.
I AM one with the Spirit.
I AM God's Spirit.

Say these words knowing that God lives inside the holy temple
of your body waiting for you to call on Him.

Got Faith?

I'm praying aren't I?
Look, I'm tired and confused,
and you're all I've got right now.
Does that answer your question?

What are you confused about?
You. Me. Everything.
I love you. What's confusing about that?
What's confusing is I feel like $#i+!

I feel like this is never gonna end.
I feel like I'm wasting my time.
I feel like nobody cares.
I feel like there's no end to this nightmare.

I feel like what little faith I have is almost gone.
I feel like I'm not gonna make it.
I feel like I want to cry, but I can't.
I feel like I won't stop crying once I start.

Now, what are you gonna do?
Love you.
Honestly, that really doesn't do anything for me.
Why not?

I don't know.
Sure you do.
I said I DON'T KNOW.
Think about it. Don't you believe I love you?

I loved you in your mother's womb.
I loved you even more when you were born.
I loved you when you lost your front teeth.
I loved you when you had your first crush.

I loved you when you first fell in love.
I loved you when he broke your heart.
I loved you when you hated yourself.
I loved you then, and I love you now.

Learn to love yourself,
and you'll learn to love me.
As long as you don't believe
that you deserve to be loved,
you won't accept my love or anyone else's.

Don't give up. I'll NEVER give up on you.
Have faith. I have faith in you.
If you don't have any faith in yourself,
have faith in me, and ask for more faith.
All you have to say is: Got faith?

Your Journal: Pampering Yourself and Soothing Your Soul

Because you deserve to be loved and pampered, consider writing a list of how you can pamper and take better care of yourself. Then, pick one a week to work on and keep adding to this list.

You might want to create your own book filled with everything that soothes your soul, like your affirmations or a photo of someone you love and maybe choose a title for it like *Well-Deserved Love*. You can use a notebook, journal, or a hardcover book with a blank cover found at art supply stores if you want to design your own cover.

Peace

Peace,
I thought, only happened in church
when we would shake hands.
As a kid, this was my favorite part of the mass.
I liked giving peace and receiving it too.
Without any strings and nothing to do.

Peace,
I really could not comprehend
since I never knew peace in my own little bed.
Flashbacks still make me feel his presence is near,
but then I remind myself that it's just my childlike fear.

Peace,
I now know, is the presence of God.
It's a great feeling of being perfectly loved.
Even though I'm still struggling with a lot of the pain,
I am wholeheartedly determined. I KNOW, I WILL WIN!

Your Journal: Seeking Out Peacefulness Every Day

What makes you feel peaceful?

Watching a sunset, taking a walk outside, being with a loved one,
or reminiscing about them?

How can you include peace in your life every day?

By including quiet time with God, pampering yourself,
or reading a good book?

Spirit of Love

I AM spirit.
I AM love.
I AM not just above.
I AM everywhere in everyone and everything you see.
Look carefully and believe, and YOU WILL see me.

I AM that gentle nudge of encouragement when no one is there.
I AM that second wind that you needed and begged for in prayer.
I AM what carries you on those days
        when you thought you'd collapse.
I AM what calms and comforts you just before power naps.
I AM inside you right now, but you're scared and can't see.
Pray and believe, and YOU WILL see me.

I AM standing right here with arms open wide.
I AM crying as you continually hide.
I AM trying to love you in all that I do.
I AM trying to tell you that I'LL ALWAYS LOVE YOU.
I AM reaching out, but you just pull away and can't see.
Look, pray and believe, and YOU WILL see me.

Your Journal: Talking to God Like He's Your Best Friend

To find God, look inside your heart and start talking to Him and telling Him everything like He's your best friend. Ask Him to keep you focused on His endless love and your healing path. Always remember that you are precious, and you are loved more than you can ever imagine. You are remarkable, and you're still here for a reason.

Consider starting a separate journal where you write everything down you want to tell God and the responses you receive from Him.

So you can begin or continue your healing journey, please also consider seeking out professional help in your community and letting trusted friends and family know you need their love and support.

See the Resources section in the back of this book.

Live

I want you to live.
I want you to love.
I want you to know
I'M INSIDE YOU
and not just above
in the clouds and the stars
but that I'm all around.

Wherever you go,
I want you to know
that I'm there.
Yes, that's ME beside you
sitting next to you in that empty chair.

I'm trying to get your attention, you see,
but you're drowning in fear,
wishing you could shed AT LEAST just one tear,
so your suffering would leave your body and soul.
And right now, you feel 10 times as old.
"No, that's not right," you think. "Then I'd be dead.
Maybe that's not such a bad idea," you said.

What's the use of suffering over and over again?
When will the agony come to an end?
Why not end it all if that's what we want to do?
Didn't you say we have free will? Aha! Now I've got you!!!

That's right. It's free will that you have,
and when I gave it to you, I was glad
because true love isn't love without freedom you see.
As much as it hurts me, I have to agree.

I hope that you'll listen to me just one more time
while I tell you I love you and how much I cry
beside you while trying to remind you again
that I've conquered suffering before and original sin,
and with your free will, we can do it together. Just let me know when.

Touched by God

Pills, or drugs, or alcohol.
Maybe I'll just do them all.
I didn't know. I couldn't think.
I only knew that this was it.

I'd reached my limit. I couldn't stand it anymore.
I only remember crying in the silence of my room.
Crying silent tears, I thought I'd fall asleep,
but then I saw Him. I saw Him when I closed my eyes.

I saw Him standing over me with streaming tears like mine.
I saw my agony in his face and eyes, and at that moment,
He gently lifted up my chin from deep within my chest,
and we were one. He was in me, and I was in Him.

He told me with his eyes He loved me.
He told me He is always with me.
He told me to remember this moment.
He told me He would love me for all eternity.

Your Journal: How Were You Touched by God?

Write about when you felt like you were touched by God.

Be

Be.
What am I supposed to be?
Whatever you want to be.
What about just being you?

Be me.
I don't want to be me.
Who do you want to be?
I want to be anyone BUT me.

Can't you just speed up the time?
I'm tired of feeling the pain of guilt that's not really mine.
I'm tired of sleepless nights all the time.
I'm tired of feeling that evil lurks deep inside.
I'm tired of nightmares where I'm never heard.
I'm tired of hiding it all from the world.

When will it stop?
When will it end?
When will it all be a distant and faint memory?
When will I FINALLY be free?

That all depends.
Depends on what?
Depends on who you want to be.

I'm not searching for the meaning of life.
What are you looking for?
Peace.

You already have that.
No, I don't.
That's because you're denying who you are —
who I created you to be.

So, who did you create me to be?
I created you to be true to yourself and me.
I created you to be mine.
I created you to BE.

Your Journal: Who and What Do You Want To Be?

"It's never too late to be what you might have been."

George Eliot, aka Mary Ann Evans (1819–1880)

Who and what do you want to be?

What If?

What if I can never learn how to have a normal relationship?
What if I'm so screwed up,
I can never have a normal relationship?
What if I never find anyone who even wants me?

What if you DO find someone who wants you?
What if you let him get to know you?
What if you tell him about what happened to you when you feel ready?

What if he wholeheartedly supports you?
What if he compassionately focuses on your feelings and needs?
What if he falls in love with you?

What if he's ready for intimacy and vulnerability,
and you push him away?
What if he refuses to let you give up?
What if he says you're the most amazing woman he's ever met?

Your Journal: Getting Rid of the Negative "What Ifs"

How can you prepare yourself to be open to meeting that special man or woman today?

Consider writing your own negative list of "What ifs" in one column and turning them into positive affirmations in another column. Every time you catch yourself saying a negative "What if," counteract it by saying, "That's wrong." Then, follow it up by saying your positive affirmation to yourself or aloud.

Pray

Pray?!?
That's it?!!
No. Pray everywhere.
What am I, a nun?

You can pray while brushing your teeth.
You can pray while washing your face.
You can pray while taking a shower.
You can pray while cooking or eating breakfast
or just having your coffee.

You can pray whenever you feel like you're losing your patience.
You can pray whenever you're stuck in traffic.
You can pray whenever you're standing in line.
You can pray whenever you feel like swearing.

You can pray at work.
You can pray at home.
You can pray at the park or on the beach.
You can pray wherever you go because I'm always there.

Choose one for now. JUST ONE.
And I PROMISE YOU, your faith will grow.
Spend time with me, and let me love you unconditionally.
Accept my love in prayer, and I will show you your destiny.

Your Journal: Loving Yourself and Embracing God's Love

Prayer is your time to practice allowing God to freely love you and embrace being loved by Him. To be open to God's love, practice loving yourself by writing a list of your good qualities and everything else you like about yourself. Read your list every day and keep adding to it.

Try spending more time listening as well as talking to Him like you would do with your best friend. Although you know you can have a discussion with God any time, make time for at least five minutes every morning and night.

Belong to the Truth

What is truth?

The truth is
that
I
love
you
MORE
than you can ever imagine.

Like the air that surrounds you wherever you go,
my infinite spirit embraces you
and
LIVES inside you.

Like a mustard seed planted in soil RAVAGED by time!

Yes, you're right, but
I
STILL
love
You,
And I STILL believe in you.
Even when you've given up hope, I'm still here!

Search for me, and you will find me.
Ask for my help, and I WILL help you.

Yes, it will be as painful as childbirth, but
I
AM
here
for
you.

Let me hold you up when you're ready to fall,
and hug you close when there's no one at all.
Turn to me. Come to me, and put your head on my shoulder.

When the world has sucked the life out of you, LET ME
breathe
life
back
into
you.

LET ME
love you perfectly because you are mine.
Belong to the truth.

Inspired by a reading on Good Friday (see John 18:37–38).

The Truth

All alone inside my room,
I grabbed another orange.
Along with my seductive knife,
my mind began to wander.

I shook my head in disbelief
when remembering dinner with a friend
and how Tim made a pass at me,
and I felt like dying once again.

Just like with my father, I pretended everything was fine.
The next day I kept running through the details in my mind.
Retracing every step, asking myself, "What did I do wrong?
What exactly did I do to make all this happen again?"

I could finally see after days
of thinking in and out of therapy.
He knew what my father did,
and like my father, he manipulated me.

As I held the knife, I heard the Lord talking in my head,
"Don't do it. Wait! At least hear me out.
Put down the knife. Please. PLEASE, put down the knife."

I put the knife down, but right away I picked it up again.
The next thing I knew, I heard, *"No. Don't! Stop. Listen!*
Hold your head in your hands and just listen. I LOVE YOU.
Maybe you can't see it. Maybe you don't feel it,
or seem to care, but you do.
And, I DO LOVE YOU."

Why? Because you deserve to be loved.
You deserve to be surrounded by people who love you like I do.
You deserve to enjoy the warmth of summer days,
and cool refreshing breezes that let me reach out and comfort you.
You deserve a soul mate to share your life and love.
You deserve all this and so much more, so put the knife down.
No, throw it away.

Kneel right now and talk to me.
That's right, just pray.
Don't worry about what to say, or how to say it.
Just talk to me like you would one of your close friends.
That's exactly what I want to be: your best friend.

Then, God whispered in the silence of my heart
four words I'll never forget: *Belong to the truth.*
And, yes, I put down the knife.

Prayer

Prayer, I know, doesn't always feel right.

Remain in my love. I beg you tonight.

A war rages inside you, and I'm right here to guide you.

Your haunting anguish tears away at your soul and leaves you wondering which way to go.

EVEN I can't stand to see you suffering sometimes.

Return to me. In your heart lies your divinity. Your only true identity.

Your Journal: Letting God Love You in the Silence of Your Heart

"Be still and know that I am God." (Psalm 46:11)

God is always with you waiting for you to allow Him to love you.

Remember, you can always reach out to God, especially when you start feeling numb, depressed, or overwhelmed.

When you're with loved ones, words aren't always necessary. Try sitting quietly with your eyes closed, while opening your heart, mind, body, and soul to God, and let Him love you in the silence of your heart. Then, write about your experience.

Redemptive Suffering

Are you kidding me?
Who am I? The virgin Mary?
Well, my name's Mary, and I'm no virgin,
but then you already knew that.

Tell me why. Why is there suffering at all?
I know we're all suffering unless we're physically dead,
so why not kill us all and let the world end.

I'll give you your answer,
but first answer ME.
Why do people, hate, kill and maim?
Why do they torture, prolonging the pain?
Why do they cheat, steal and lie?
Why do they want a bigger piece of the pie?

Why can't they be happy with all they've got?
Why can't those that have, help all the "have-nots?"
Don't get me wrong. It's okay to want more,
but it's certainly not right just to hoard.

Then there are talents.
I gave everyone some.
To some I gave more. Others only have one.

How many people do you know, tell me now,
that have found and really use the talents they have?
How many have done so and are eternally glad
to go to work every day and get paid
for what they feel is essentially play?

You know the answer, and, of course, I do, too,
because so many come to me unhappy like you.
So, tell me why. Why is there suffering at all?
You know you're all suffering unless we're physically dead,
so why aren't you doing something about it before the world ends?

Inspired by Fr. William J. O'Malley, S.J.'s book,

Redemptive Suffering: Understanding Suffering, Living with It,
and Growing Through It
(New York: The Crossroad Publishing Company, 1997. Print).

Your Journal: Who Inspires You?
and
What Can You Learn from Them?

Like any good father or mother, our divine creator shares our unjust suffering and keeps reaching out to pull us out of the darkness, knowing that our triumphs over evil will inspire others, so our victories become lights in the darkness transforming the world.

Write about who inspires you and what you can learn from them.

Conquering Evil

What are you talking about?
What do you mean?
I'm not a saint.
I'm just trying to heal,
and YOU of all people should know how I feel.

That's what I mean. Evil wins whenever you run and just hide.
I know it'll be the hardest thing that I've asked you to do,
but you'll never find peace if you don't follow through.
Whenever you feel alone and afraid, please remember,
that I AM the good that you need at that moment in time.

Then, come to me and unload your burdens and fears.
Together we'll walk, or I'll carry you through.
It really doesn't matter what words you use.
Know that I LOVE YOU. You are eternally mine,
and I'm right here beside you. LET ME be your guide.

I am your Father:
Your strength, your perseverance, your source of peace.
Lay your head on my shoulder,
and LET ME gently hold you and rock you in my arms once again
while my heart cries with yours, and we're one in your pain.

Then, don't get discouraged, when I tell you to fight.
Know that I am always beside you, helping you fight for your life.
I know that you're tired and overwhelmed now,
and you're thinking: Fighting, but how?
Fight evil with good. You're still confused. I'll explain.

I am inside you and you are in me.
I am your strength: your divinity.
I am the life you will find in your truth.
Seek out good people, and I will send them to you.
Trust them, and they will help you find the way.
All I ask is that you be the "good people" someone prays for one day.

Inspired by Romans 12:21, "Do not be conquered by evil, but conquer evil with good."

Your Journal: Conquer the Lies of the Criminals Who Violated You

"For whoever is begotten by God conquers the world.
And the victory that conquers the world is our faith."

(1 John 5:4)

Keep conquering the lies of the criminal(s) who violated you and brainwashed you into believing everything that happened was your fault when it was ALL their fault. Belong to the truth, NOT the lies.

Write the sentences below 10 times each, or make up your own to add or substitute.

I deserve a better life.

I deserve to live a life that far surpasses my hopes and dreams.

I am guilt-free because the criminal who hurt me is to blame. None of it is mine.

I am not ashamed because the criminal who hurt me owns all the shame.

Your Destiny

Healing is your destiny.
First, you must find your true self,
and learn to love yourself,
unconditionally,
as God loves you.

For to know God is to know love,
and to know love is to accept love.
And to accept love, you
MUST BELIEVE yourself worthy of love.

Don't worry how long it might take.
God's more than willing to wait.
He loved you long before you were born,
and longs for you to receive His love and so much more.

Find your passion, and you will find your mission.
Find your mission, and you will find God.
Find God, and you will find peace.

His will is our peace,
and our peace is in Him.

Your Journal: Co-Creating Your Destiny with God

Your destiny begins with what you believe.

What do you believe now about your destiny?

What is the truth you should believe about your destiny?

The Passion

My mission was following the will of God.
THE PASSION was My mission.
Find your passion, and you will find your mission.
Follow your mission, and you will find God's peace.

A special gift for you: Musically, spark your spirit
with a **FREE** copy of my song,
"When Life Gets You Down, Get Up!"
See the last page of this book for details.

Resources

If you encounter problems contacting any resources below, please consult our Website, DivinefulnessPublishing.com/resources, for updated information or search the Internet for these organizations by name.

Contact your local domestic violence program, shelter, or rape crisis center to learn about free cell phone donation programs.

Remember that "corded" phones are more private and less interceptable than cordless phones or analog cell phones.

Be aware you may not be able to reach 911 using an Internet phone or Internet-based phone service, so you may need to be prepared to use another phone to call 911.

24/7 Teen Dating Violence and Domestic Violence Hotlines—Info and Referral Services

U.S. National Teen Dating Violence Hotline
Website: loveisrespect.org
24/7 Online Chat with Peers or Call (866) 331-9474

Domestic Violence National Hotline/
Linea Nacional Sobre La Violencia Domestica
English Website: thehotline.org
Spanish Website: espanol.thehotline.org
Multilingual: (800) 799-SAFE (7233)
TTY for the Deaf: (800) 787-3224
TTY Para Los Sordos: (800) 787-3224

24/7 Sexual Assault Hotlines

RAINN (Rape, Abuse & Incest National Network)
English Website: hotline.rainn.org/online/terms-of-service.jsp
Spanish Website: hotline.rainn.org/es/terms-of-service.jsp
24/7 Online Chat or Call to Find Counseling
2000 L Street, NW Suite 406
Washington, DC 20036
(800) 656-HOPE (4673)

1in6 (Researchers' Statistical Estimate for Men)
Website: 1in6.org
24/7 Online Helpline for Men & Anonymous Online Groups
Info and resources available for loved ones and care providers

U.S. Dept of Veteran Affairs
Website: ptsd.va.gov/public/where-to-get-help.asp
24/7 Online Chat or Call to Find Counseling
Washington, DC Regional Office
1722 I Street NW
Washington, DC 20421
(800) 273-TALK (8255)

Other Victim Assistance Resources

Know Your IX
Website: knowyourix.org
knowyourix@gmail.com

When encountering sexual harassment, Know Your IX provides
helpful information for US college students about their rights under
Title IX. It's not just about sports.

SNAP (Survivors Network of Those Abused by Priests)
Website: snapnetwork.org
P.O. Box 6416
Chicago, IL 60680-6416
Call to Find Counseling
(877) SNAPHEALS (877) 762-7432

SNAP is the nation's largest, oldest and most active support group for women and men wounded by religious authority figures of all faiths (priests, ministers, bishops, deacons, nuns and others).

They are an independent and confidential organization with no connections to any organized religion or religious hierarchy.

U.S. Crime Victims' Compensation Overview
Website: ovc.gov/pubs/crimevictimsfundfs/intro.html#vc

U.S. Office for Victims of Crime
Website: ovc.gov

U.S. Resource Map of Crime Victims Services and Information
Website: ojp.gov/ovc/map.html
U.S. Department of Justice
810 Seventh Street, NW, Eighth Floor
Washington, DC 20531
Phone: (202) 307-5983
Fax: (202) 514-6383

Latest Medical Research

National Institute of Mental Health
Website: nimh.nih.gov/health/topics/post-traumatic-stress-disorder-ptsd/index.shtml
Mailing address: Science Writing, Press, and Dissemination Branch
6001 Executive Boulevard, Room 8184, MSC 9663
Bethesda, MD 20892-9663
Local: (301) 443-4513 / Toll-free: (866) 615-6464
TTY: (301) 443-8431 / TTY Toll-Free: (866) 415-8051
Email: nimhinfo@nih.gov

Afterword

God's unconditional love, priceless faith, and infinite graces saved my life. Grounded by His gift of faith, nurtured by my mother, the coping skills I learned in counseling and group therapy sessions transformed me from a suicidal incest victim to an empowered survivor.

In November 2004, the darkness crept into my life once more. The only friend I had nearby, who was married and like a brother to me, made a pass at me knowing that I was a survivor of childhood sexual abuse. Suicidal thoughts started creeping in again. I was living at the YMCA in Chicago's Gold Coast in a room the size of a large walk-in closet and working as a security guard in a River North condo building where a resident was trying to get me fired for doing my job.

My life was miserable, but by the grace of God, I persevered. The darkness overcame me many times back then, but I kept holding on to my faith in God and I wouldn't let go. I couldn't afford an iPod or an Internet connection, so I listened to the radio a lot. In 2005, when I wrote the poems in this book, Kelly Clarkson's song "Breakaway" was still popular and became my theme song. Whenever I heard "Breakaway," it catapulted me over the rainbow.

Recently, long after I wrote this book, I struggled through the worst depression I ever experienced. My mind, senses, and spirit constantly wrestled with the bleak darkness, and my only consolation came during prayer. I felt myself slipping away and disappearing, regressing to my tormented childhood days never to return.

Thank God I met William Rosado, another survivor, who wisely assessed I had not completely forgiven my deceased father or myself as I told him I already did. He helped me achieve a miraculous breakthrough on July 7, 2014, my deceased step-sister Mary's birthday. Also sexually abused by our biological father, I felt she saved my life and expunged my guilt for not finding her before she passed away.

William reminded me of the power of God's love while carefully guiding and counseling me through completely forgiving my father and myself. However, I had to finish the process on my own in private between God and me. Determined, I had no idea how it would end. After endless tears and painfully excavating the depths of my soul, I finally achieved absolute forgiveness for my father and me. Beaten, torn, and tattered, my heart exploded, and my post-traumatic stress (PTS) became history. Thanks be to God!

While I wholeheartedly support survivors whether they seek justice in court or not, I believe justice and forgiveness are independently possible. As a part of their healing process, survivors determine what they need to do to resurrect their spirit. My mission is serving them on their healing journey.

Today, I am a happy and peaceful person. Every sexual assault survivor deserves to live a happy and peaceful life. Maybe you don't feel like it right now, but you are in control of your life. You and God, Nature, or whatever you call your higher power, together you can do anything.

After I decided to publish this book, I thought about survivors visiting our Website. I wanted to console them somehow, especially if they were having a bad day. I kept thinking about the old *Cheers* TV series, and how it had such a fun and cheerful theme song. That's what I wanted: a feel-good theme song for our Website.

By the looks on their faces, I knew the few people I told about my idea didn't think it was so great. I just couldn't give up on it, so I started praying for it in the summer of 2008. The words came to me gradually. It wasn't until right before Christmas that year that I finished the lyrics.

For the longest time, I knew the song was incomplete because it had no heart and soul. A stanza was missing. I finally understood after the words came to me. God held back the stanza, not because he was being stingy, but because I had to learn to live the words on my own before I could write them. I had to be authentic.

In 2009, I asked my friend Shyvone Blunt if she would record our Website theme song for me, "When Life Gets You Down, Get Up!" I didn't even know if she could sing. Something told me to ask her, and wow, can she sing! God works in mysterious ways because Shyvone was estranged from God at the time. He loves drama, too, because I don't know anything about music. The words and the music just started coming to me one day, and more songs keep coming. I wrote a rap song a short time later.

What's next? I'm working on a book about self-love and more songs are coming, too, and eventually a CD with inspiring and uplifting songs. Then, there's a children's coloring book and a comic book series for child sexual abuse survivors. Additionally, my future plans include visiting women in prison and kids at juvenile detention centers.

The lyrics for our Website theme song, "When Life Gets You Down, Get Up!" follow the "Connect with Mary Vasquez" page. Listen to an audio clip of the song now at divinefulns.us/MarysSongClip.

Excluding free offers, for every book you purchase, I will donate $1 to the YWCA for sexual assault counseling. Join our email list now, and this song is yours for **FREE**. Go directly to our Website at divinefulns.us/LpfgMarysFreeSong, or scan the QR code on the last page of this book.

Help me write my next book, *Loving Me 101: Loving My Divinefulness,* and receive advance notice about future online retreats. For details, see the "Connect with Mary Vasquez" page.

Currently, sexual assault survivors and other crime victims do not have enforceable rights like defendants. This injustice causes survivors and their families to endure needless suffering. Please consider signing a petition for the US Constitutional Amendment HJ Res 106 found at nvcap.org and encourage others to join their voices in supporting all crime victims.

Did you know that as early as 1993, the American Psychological Association published a report referencing 45 clinical studies that found PTS often occurred in child sexual abuse survivors? The PTS experienced by survivors of childhood sexual abuse mirrors the PTS war veterans suffer, so please be forgiving and gentle with yourself or your loved one.

Remember, you are loved. You are precious. You are remarkable, and you're still here for a reason. Belong to the truth.

About the Author

Born, raised, and still living in Chicago, Illinois, Mary Vasquez is a survivor of childhood sexual abuse on a mission to serve people with life-altering experiences. Her biological father sexually abused her from about the age of five until she turned 13. Mary says she has been blessed with the remarkable experience and privilege of writing a book she never wanted to write.

Her first book and passion for spirituality inspired her to launch Divinefulness Publishing, Inc. Mary looks forward to publishing more spiritual books by and for people with life-altering experiences, loved ones, and care providers, such as therapists, clergy, employees and volunteers of nonprofit organizations.

Listen to her podcast, ***Beautiful Me: Loving My Divinefulness,*** at divinefulnesspublishing.com/podcast. See the next page to find out where you can connect with Mary, so you receive advance notice about her online retreats.

She can't wait to finish her next book and produce more music that God sends her way. Mary encourages you to share your thoughts about her book and Website theme song, "When Life Gets You Down, Get Up!" Read the inspirational lyrics after the next page.

Mary serves on the Planning Committee for the Chicagoland Trauma Informed Congregation Network, an effort by the Substance Abuse and Mental Health Services Administration (SAMHSA), University of Illinois Hospital, and Advocate Health. She said, "It's invigorating to be involved with others passionate about serving people with life-altering experiences."

Connect with Mary Vasquez

For inspiration and love in a safe place, find us on Facebook at Divinefulness Publishing and on Twitter @DivinefulnsPub.

To stay in touch with Mary, join her on Facebook at Divinefulness Mary, and on Twitter @DivinefulnsMary. Find her on Pinterest at DivinefulnsMary.

Follow Mary on social media, so you can help her write her next book, *Loving Me 101: Loving My Divinefulness,* and receive advance notice about future online retreats.

Listen to her podcast, *Beautiful Me: Loving My Divinefulness,* at divinefulnesspublishing.com/podcast

Survivors, loved ones, and care providers should email her at mary@divinefulnesspublishing.com.

If you prefer snail mail, send your letter to

Mary Vasquez
Divinefulness Publishing, Inc.
P.O. Box 34288
Chicago, IL 60634

For speaking engagements, media inquiries, and all other business matters, please be sure to include "Business" as the first word in your subject before emailing her at mary@divinefulnesspublishing.com.

When Life Gets You Down, Get Up! (Song Lyrics)

Don't listen to the voices in your head
convincing you that your dreams are dead.
Tell them. Right here. Right now. They're wrong.
Go back and say, "No way. I'm strong!"

When life gets you down, get up.
When life gets you down, get up. When life…
When life gets you down, get up.
When life gets you down, get up.
When life gets you down, get up. When life…
When life gets you down, get up.
When life gets you down, get up.

When your friends laugh and look at you
And say, "Your dreams won't ever come true,"
Tell them. Right here. Right now. They're wrong.
Get out! Get out! And move along.

When life gets you down, get up.
When life gets you down, get up. When life…
When life gets you down, get up.
When life gets you down, get up.
When life gets you down, get up. When life…
When life gets you down, get up.
When life gets you down, get up.

When you're settled in your newfound life,
Things are goin' great and there's no more strife.
A good friend comes along
'n then you feel betrayed.
When you want to quit and hide away.
Feelin' like you can't take life no more.
Get down on your knees 'n keep hittin' that floor.

When life kicks you down, pray hard. Pray hard! Pray hard 'n
find the light!

When you listen and you pray some more
Real soon you'll find that open door.
Just keep prayin' hard; keep hittin' that floor.
Tell God. Right here. Right now. I'm yours.
I'll give you all of me: mind, body, and soul.
He'll pave a way and show you a new role.

When God lifts you up, give thanks.
Give thanks! Give thanks and be the light!
When God lifts you up, give thanks.
Give thanks! Give thanks and be the light!
When God lifts you up, give thanks.
Give thanks! Give thanks and be the light!

Preview a song clip from "When Life Gets You Down, Get Up!"
on our Website at divinefulns.us/MarysSongClip.

Excluding free offers, for every book you purchase, I will donate $1 to the YWCA for sexual assault counseling.

Join our email list, and this song is yours for **FREE**. Go directly to our Website at divinefulns.us/LpfgMarysFreeSong.

Help Mary write her next book, *Loving Me 101: Loving My Divinefulness,* and receive advance notice about future online retreats. For details, see the "Connect with Mary Vasquez" page.

www.ingramcontent.com/pod-product-compliance
Lightning Source LLC
Chambersburg PA
CBHW031606040426